TYRANNOSAURUS

AND OTHER GIANT MEAT-EATERS

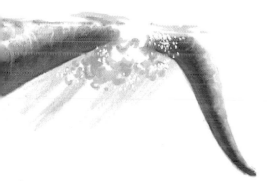

Prehistoric World

TYRANNOSAURUS
AND OTHER GIANT MEAT-EATERS

VIRGINIA
SCHOMP

BENCHMARK BOOKS

MARSHALL CAVENDISH
NEW YORK

DINOSAURS LIVED MILLIONS OF YEARS AGO. EVERYTHING WE KNOW ABOUT THEM—HOW THEY LOOKED, WALKED, ATE, FOUGHT, MATED, AND RAISED THEIR YOUNG—COMES FROM EDUCATED GUESSES BY THE SCIENTISTS WHO DISCOVER AND STUDY FOSSILS. THE INFORMATION IN THIS BOOK IS BASED ON WHAT MOST SCIENTISTS BELIEVE RIGHT NOW. TOMORROW OR NEXT WEEK OR NEXT YEAR, NEW DISCOVERIES COULD LEAD TO NEW IDEAS. SO KEEP YOUR EYES AND EARS OPEN FOR NEWS FLASHES FROM THE PREHISTORIC WORLD!

With thanks to Brent H. Breithaupt, Director of The Geological Museum, University of Wyoming, for his expert reading of the manuscript.

Benchmark Books
Marshall Cavendish
99 White Plains Road
Tarrytown, New York 10591-9001
www.marshallcavendish.com

© Marshall Cavendish Corporation 2003

Library of Congress Cataloging-in-Publication Data

Schomp, Virginia.
  Tyrannosaurus and other giant meat-eaters / by Virginia Schomp.
    p. cm. -- (Prehistoric world)
Includes index and bibliographical references.
Summary: An introduction to the physical characteristics and habits of
Tyrannosaurus rex and other meat-eating dinosaurs.
  ISBN 0-7614-1020-1
1. Tyrannosaurus rex--Juvenile literature. 2. Predatory animals--Juvenile literature.
[1. Tyrannosaurus rex. 2. Dinosaurs.] I. Title.
QE862.S3 S387 2002
567.912'9--dc21   2001052409

Front cover: *Tyrannosaurus rex*
Back cover: *Daspletosaurus*

Photo Credits:
Cover illustration: The Natural History Museum, London / John Sibbick

The illustrations and photographs in this book are used by the permission and through the courtesy of:
Corbis: Layne Kennedy, 12 (top); Philip Gould, 24. *Marshall Cavendish Corporation:* 2-3, 10, 11, 12 (bottom), 15, 16, 17, 18, 19, 20-21, 22, 23, 25, back cover. *The Natural History Museum, London:* Orbis, 8; John Sibbick, 14.

Map and Dinosaur Family Tree by Robert Romagnoli

Printed in Hong Kong
1 3 5 6 4 2

For Rusty, Tyler, Miranda, and Chandler

Contents

TIME OF THE TYRANTS
8

TIME LINE: THE AGE OF DINOSAURS
9

DINOSAUR DAYS
13

MAP: THE LATE CRETACEOUS WORLD
13

TYRANNOSAUR WAYS
17

WHERE ARE THE DINOSAURS?
25

DINOSAUR FAMILY TREE
26

GLOSSARY
28

FIND OUT MORE
29

INDEX
31

TIME OF THE TYRANTS

Hungry T. rex *attacks a defenseless duck-billed dinosaur.*

Northern America, millions of years ago. A herd of duck-billed dinosaurs drink from a lake's muddy waters. Suddenly a fierce *Tyrannosaurus rex* lunges from the nearby forest. Hooting in alarm, the herd scatters. Amid the noise and confusion, the *T. rex* zeros in on one fleeing dinosaur and quickly overtakes it. Baring its sharp fangs, the killer chomps down. Neck broken, the duckbill falls. As it lies stunned and helpless, the *Tyrannosaurus* starts feeding.

Huge and incredibly powerful, *Tyrannosaurus* was the most fearsome predator the world has ever known. Even its name stands tall: *Tyrannosaurus rex* means "king of the tyrant lizards." This king ruled the earth about 65 million years ago, at the end of the Age of Dinosaurs.

Imagine a world teeming with dinosaurs. There are hundreds of different kinds. Some are deadly meat-eaters like *Tyrannosaurus*, while others munch on plants. There are dinosaurs with two legs, with four legs, with hoofs, beaks, feathers, and body armor. Some are taller than a five-story building, some no bigger than a chicken.

To keep all these creatures straight, paleontologists (scientists who study prehistoric life) divide them into groups. *Tyrannosaurus* belongs to a group

The Age of Dinosaurs

Dinosaurs walked the earth during the Mesozoic era, also known as the Age of Dinosaurs. The Mesozoic era lasted from about 250 million to 65 million years ago. It is divided into three periods: the Triassic, Jurassic, and Cretaceous.

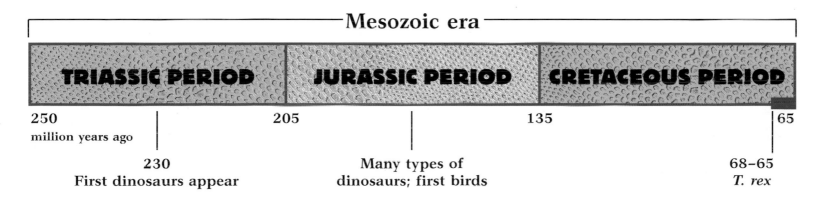

ALLOSAURUS
(ah-luh-SORE-us)
When: Late Jurassic,
   140–135 million years ago
Where: western United
States
◆ **Top predator of Jurassic
   period**
◆ **Probably hunted in packs**

An Allosaurus *smile was a scary sight—this fierce meat-eater had huge jaws lined with sharp, saw-edged teeth.*

of dinosaurs called theropods. All theropods were two-legged meat-eaters. On page 26, you can see how *T. rex* and the other giant theropods in this book fit into the dinosaur family tree.

FANG-FLASHING FAMILIES

Most of the earliest theropods were small-fry. Fierce but tiny *Compsognathus*, which lived way back 150 million years ago, was only the size of a house cat.

Then along came the giants. *Allosaurus*, with its huge jaws, stabbing teeth, and meat-hook claws, was the two-ton terror of the Late Jurassic period. But scariest of all were the "tyrant lizards" of the Cretaceous period, the tyrannosaur family.

TYRANNOSAURUS
(tie-ran-oh-SORE-us)
**When: Late Cretaceous,
68–65 million years ago
Where: western United
States and Canada**
• As long as a tractor trailer
• As tall as a 2-story house

T. rex may have been a good swimmer that could chase down its meals both on land and in the water.

CLAWS AND JAWS

One paleontologist described Tyrannosaurus's *long, sharp, saw-edged teeth as "deadly bananas."*

Teeth as long and sharp as steak knives. Jaws more powerful than a crocodile's. A mouth so huge it could have swallowed a grown man in one bite (luckily, none were available back then). Along with these impressive weapons, *Tyrannosaurus* had a forty-foot-long body, strong back legs armed with deadly claws, and a long muscular tail, which it carried straight out behind. The only things out of place on this colossal killing machine were the arms. Like most theropods, *Tyrannosaurus* had ridiculously short arms—too short even to reach its mouth.

No one knows how Daspletosaurus *and the other giant meat-eating dinosaurs used their odd-looking little arms.*

DASPLETOSAURUS
(das-plee-toh-SORE-us)
When: Late Cretaceous, 75–70 million years ago
Where: Canada
- **Weighed up to 3 tons— as much as 12 tigers**
- **Fewer, larger teeth than other tyrannosaurs**

DINOSAUR DAYS

Dinosaurs walked the earth a very long time—about 165 million years. During all that time, the face of the earth saw dramatic changes. At the beginning of the Mesozoic era, the earth had one huge landmass, surrounded by a giant sea. Over the centuries, continents broke apart, oceans rose and fell, and mountains and islands formed. By the end of the Cretaceous period, the world was starting to look like it does today. But if you could travel back in time 65 million years, you'd still see some startling differences.

WELCOME TO CRETACEOUS PARK!

Your time machine lands in what will one day be the western United States. You are standing on the shores of an inland ocean. In the Late Cretaceous

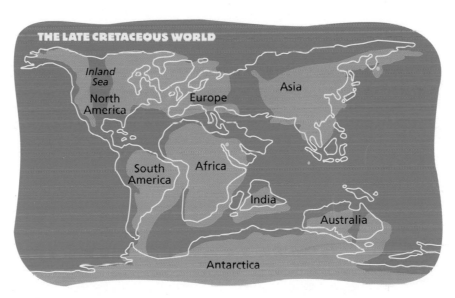

The earth's surface is always moving very, very slowly. The yellow outlines on this map show the shape of the modern continents; the green shading shows their position around 65 million years ago.

It was a jungle out there in Cretaceous times, with evergreen trees, shrubs, ferns, and moss covering the earth.

Duck-billed dinosaurs had rows of rough teeth perfect for grinding up tough leaves and twigs.

period, this shallow sea reaches from the top to the bottom of North America, cutting the continent in half.

The air is warm and sticky. A lush green forest stretches as far as the eye can see. Flowering shrubs and trees also cover the land. There are many types of dinosaurs dining on this vast salad bar. You may see herds of duck-bills—four-legged plant-eaters with rough, grinding teeth—along with heavy, horned bulldozers like *Triceratops*.

Pterosaurs (TEHR-uh-sores) were not dinosaurs but lived at the same time. These winged reptiles were the largest animals that ever flew.

Other animals share the earth with the dinosaurs. Small furry mammals and little lizards scurry across the forest floor, and ferocious meat-eating reptiles swim the seas. The skies are filled with birds and pterosaurs—flying reptiles with wings that can be as wide as a fighter jet's. Watching over all these creatures are the big hungry eyes of the new king on the block, *Tyrannosaurus.*

TYRANNOSAUR WAYS

Some paleontologists call *Tyrannosaurus* and its giant cousins "land sharks." Few creatures could survive an attack by these colossal biting machines. We don't know for sure how *T. rex* snagged its meals, but it may have sneaked up on a big plant-eating dinosaur, then charged out in a burst of power and speed. One bite from a *Tyrannosaurus*'s powerful jaws could tear out a five-hundred-pound chunk of meat. The killer swallowed its bloody mouthfuls whole. If it broke a tooth chomping down on bone, no problem— a new one soon grew in to replace it.

Predators like Carcharodontosaurus *may have had spots, stripes, or other patterns to help them blend into their surroundings.*

CARCHARODONTOSAURUS
(kar-kar-oh-DON-tuh-sore-us)
When: Middle Cretaceous, 115–90 million years ago
Where: North Africa
• As big as *Tyrannosaurus*
• Jagged teeth like a great white shark's

Discovered in 1995, Giganotosaurus *may have been bigger than* Tyrannosaurus, *but it had smaller teeth and a much smaller brain.*

Some scientists object to this view of *Tyrannosaurus* as the world's biggest, baddest hunter. They think that the king of dinosaurs was too slow and heavy to chase its meals. Instead, they say, *Tyrannosaurus* was a scavenger, feeding on the bodies of already-dead animals. Others guess that *T. rex* was both—hunting when it could, sniffing out "leftovers" when fresh flesh was unavailable.

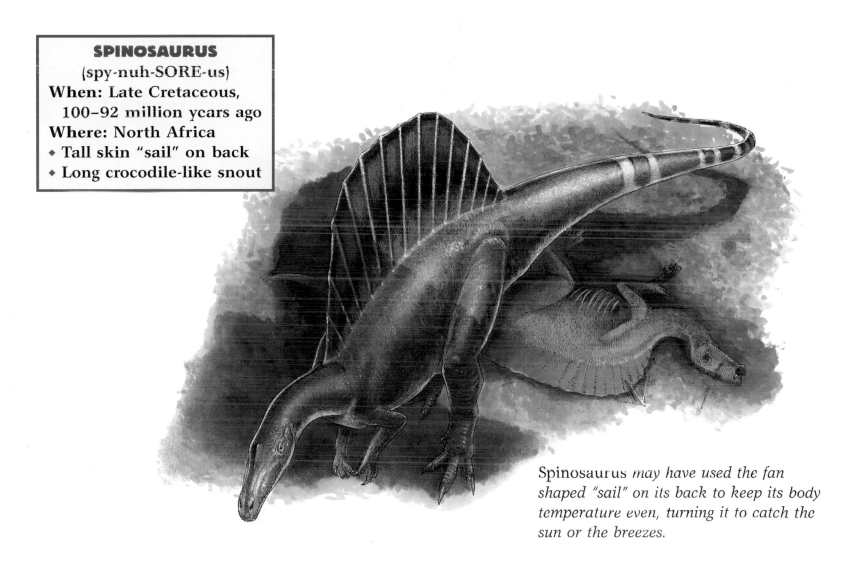

SPINOSAURUS
(spy-nuh-SORE-us)
When: Late Cretaceous,
    100–92 million years ago
Where: North Africa
• **Tall skin "sail" on back**
• **Long crocodile-like snout**

Spinosaurus *may have used the fan shaped "sail" on its back to keep its body temperature even, turning it to catch the sun or the breezes.*

TARBOSAURUS
(tar-boh-SORE-us)
When: Late Cretaceous,
 71–68 million years ago
Where: Mongolia and China
◆ Largest known meat-eater from Asia
◆ Immense head with daggerlike fangs

MORE MEAT-EATER MYSTERIES

Movies usually show fang-flashing, scenery-smashing *T. rex* as a loner. But some paleontologists believe that these predators hunted in packs. Some even think that older and younger *Tyrannosaurus* may have lived together in small groups.

Bite marks and broken bones in fossils show that tyrannosaurs like Tarbosaurus may have fought each other—probably over food, mates, and hunting grounds.

How did *T. rex* parents care for their young? What was life like in a tyrannosaur "family"? Scientists haven't found enough fossils yet to solve these mysteries. For now, the answers to these and other secrets of the giant two-legged meat-eaters lie buried back in the Age of Dinosaurs.

NANOTYRANNUS
(nan-oh-tie-RAN-us)
When: Late Cretaceous,
  69–65 million years ago
Where: Montana
◆ **One-third the size of *T. rex***
◆ **Name means "dwarf tyrant"**

Some paleontologists think that Nanotyrannus *was a young* Tyrannosaurus, *others that it was a small cousin of the king of predators.*

The fossils of several Albertosaurus *have been found buried together—perhaps a clue that this tyrannosaur lived in "family" groups.*

ALBERTOSAURUS
(al-ber-tuh-SORE-us)
When: Late Cretaceous,
  80–68 million years ago
Where: western United States and
  Canada
◆ Fierce, slightly smaller relative of
  Tyrannosaurus
◆ Strong jaws and large curved teeth

DIGGING UP DINOSAURS

No one has ever seen a dinosaur. So how do we know so much about them? Sometimes when an animal dies and becomes buried in sand or mud, its bones slowly change to rock. These hardened remains are called fossils. Teeth, nests, eggs—even dinosaur poop—also can become fossilized. So can imprints left in the ground millions of years ago by skin, footprints, feathers, and plants. Paleontologists study all these fossils. Using the clues they gather, these "dinosaur detectives" work to unravel the mysteries of dinosaur life.

When paleontologists are lucky enough to find a nearly complete dinosaur skeleton, they may share it with the world by displaying it in a museum.

"Sue" at the Field Museum in Chicago is the largest and most complete T. rex *ever found.*

WHERE ARE THE DINOSAURS?

About 65 million years ago, the dinosaurs became extinct—every last one of them died out. What caused this mysterious disappearance? Some scientists guess that a giant asteroid crashed into the earth. The collision sent up a huge cloud of dust that blocked the sun, chilling temperatures and killing plants and animals. Others believe that erupting volcanoes or dropping sea levels may have wiped out the dinosaurs.

There are also paleontologists who say that birds are the modern descendants of the ancient theropods. If that's the case, *T. rex*—or at least its small, feathered relatives—is still with us today.

Dinosaur Family Tree

ORDER   All dinosaurs are divided into two large groups, based on the shape and position of their hipbones. Saurischians had forward-pointing hipbones.

SUBORDER   Theropods were two-legged meat-eating dinosaurs.

INFRAORDER   Tetanurans had stiffened (not flexible) tails.

FAMILY   A family includes one or more types of closely related dinosaurs.

GENUS   Every dinosaur has a two-word name. The first word tells us what genus, or type, of dinosaur it is.

SPECIES   The genus plus the second part of a dinosaur's name tell us its species — the group of very similar animals it belongs to. *Tyrannosaurus rex* (often abbreviated *T. rex*) is the best-known species of *Tyrannosaurus* — and the only dinosaur commonly called by both its genus and species name.

Scientists organize all living things into groups, according to features shared.
This chart shows the groupings of the giant meat-eaters in this book.

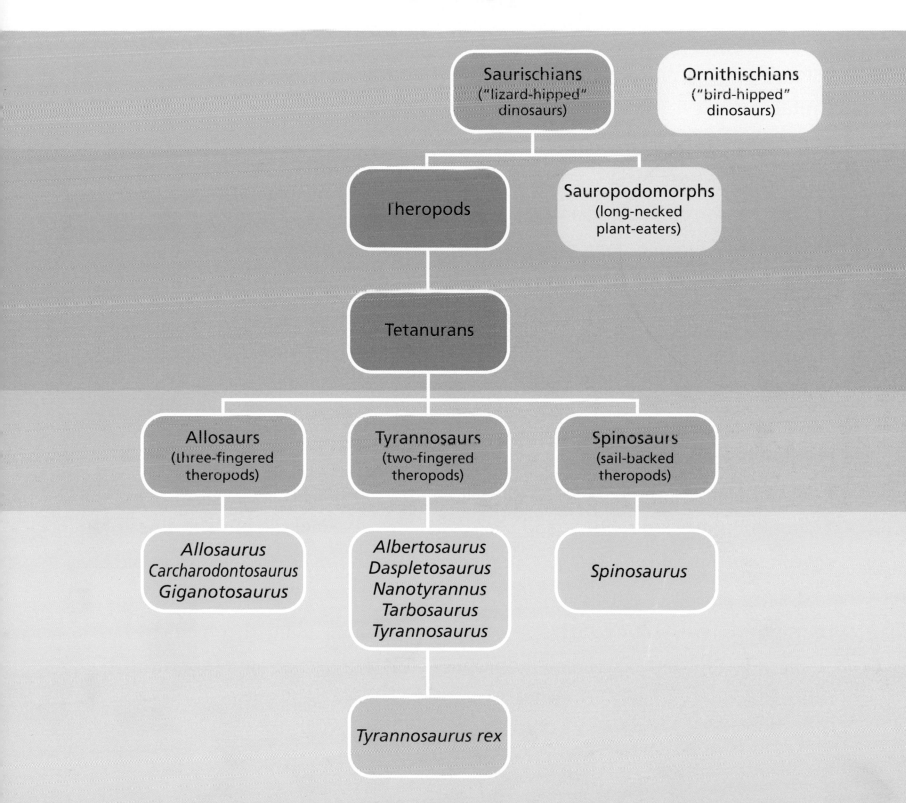

Glossary

asteroid: a very small planet or fragment of a planet orbiting the sun

Cretaceous (krih-TAY-shus) **period:** the time period from about 135 million to 65 million years ago, in which *Tyrannosaurus* and most of the other giant meat-eating dinosaurs lived

extinct: no longer existing; an animal is extinct when every one of its kind has died

fossils: the hardened remains or traces of animals or plants that lived many thousands or millions of years ago

mammals: animals that are warm-blooded, breathe air, and nurse their young with milk; humans are mammals

paleontologist (pay-lee-on-TAH-luh-jist)**:** a scientist who studies fossils to learn about dinosaurs and other forms of prehistoric life

predator: an animal that hunts and kills other animals for food

reptiles: animals that have scaly skin and, in most cases, lay eggs; crocodiles, turtles, and dinosaurs are reptiles, and some scientists also include birds in this group

scavenger: a meat-eater that feeds on animals that have already died from old age, disease, attack, or other causes

theropod: a group of two-legged meat-eating dinosaurs; many theropods had sharp teeth, back legs ending in four toes with sharp claws, and short arms

tyrant: a cruel and powerful ruler

Find Out More

Books

Cohen, Daniel. *Tyrannosaurus Rex and Other Cretaceous Meat-Eaters*. Minneapolis: Capstone Press, 1996.

Dixon, Dougal. *Dougal Dixon's Amazing Dinosaurs: The Fiercest, the Tallest, the Toughest, the Smallest*. Honesdale, PA: Boyds Mills, 2000.

The Humongous Book of Dinosaurs. New York: Stewart, Tabori, and Chang, 1997.

Lindsay, William. *On the Trail of Incredible Dinosaurs*. New York: DK Publishing, 1998.

Marshall, Chris, ed. *Dinosaurs of the World*. 11 vols. New York: Marshall Cavendish, 1999.

Rodriguez, K. S. *Tyrannosaurus Rex*. Austin, TX: Raintree Steck-Vaughn, 2000.

On-Line Sources*

Dinorama at http://www.nationalgeographic.com/dinorama/frame.html

Get the latest news on dinosaur discoveries at this National Geographic Society site.

Kinetosaurs at http://www.childrensmuseum.org/kinetosaur

Inspired by a traveling museum exhibit of moving dinosaur art, this site sponsored by the Children's Museum of Indianapolis gives step-by-step instructions for making dinosaur sculptures and other projects. Also includes fact sheets and printouts on *Tyrannosaurus* and other prehistoric creatures.

Sue at the Field Museum at http://www.fmnh.org/sue

Check out facts and photos relating to "Sue," the largest and most complete *T. rex* skeleton ever found. This website of the Field Museum in Chicago includes pages you can print out to make your own flip book of a *T. rex* in action.

UW Geological Museum Tour at http://www.uwyo.edu/geomuseum/Tour.htm

Tour the University of Wyoming Geological Museum, where exhibits include a giant fanged *T. rex* skull and "Big Al," a 25-foot-long junior *Allosaurus*.

Zoom Dinosaurs at http://www.zoomdinosaurs.com

This colorful, entertaining site from Enchanted Learning Software includes a world of information on dinosaur-related topics: dinosaur myths, records, behavior, and fossils; dinosaur fact sheets; quizzes, puzzles, printouts, and crafts; tips on writing a school report; and more.

*Website addresses sometimes change. For more on-line sources, check with the media specialist at your local library.

Index

Age of Dinosaurs. *See* Mesozoic era

Albertosaurus, 23

Allosaurus, 10, 11

Carcharodontosaurus, 17

Compsognathus, 11

Cretaceous period, 9, 11, 13–16

Daspletosaurus, 12

duck-billed dinosaurs, 8, 15

extinction, 25

fossils, 22, 24

Giganotosaurus, 18

Jurassic period, 11

Mesozoic era, 9, 13, 22

Nanotyrannus, 22

paleontologists, 9, 17, 21, 24, 25

pterosaurs, 16

Spinosaurus, 19

Tarbosaurus, 20–21

theropods, 11, 12, 25

Triceratops, 15

Tyrannosaurus
    hunting and feeding, 8–9, 11, 17, 19, 21
    living in groups, 21–22
    meaning of name, 9
    what it looked like, 11, 12
    when it lived, 9, 11

Virginia Schomp grew up in a quiet suburban town in northeastern New Jersey, where eight-ton duck-billed dinosaurs once roamed. In first grade she discovered that she loved books and writing, and in sixth grade she was named "class bookworm," because she always had her nose in a book. Today she is a freelance author who has written more than thirty books for young readers on topics including careers, animals, ancient cultures, and modern history. Ms. Schomp lives in the Catskill Mountain region of New York with her husband, Richard, and their son, Chip.